THE ALL-IN-ONE PRINTING WORKBOOK FOR KIDS

145 FUN PAGES TO MASTER WRITING SKILLS IN JUST 15 MINUTES A DAY WITH JOKES, SCIENCE FACTS, REAL PROMPTS & MORE

BY KHAULA MUBASHER

Your Free Gift

As a way of saying thanks for your purchase, I'm offering the "Bold and Easy Coloring book, "Silly Sentence Handwriting Game," and Unlimited Handwriting Practice Sheets, FREE to my readers.

To get instant access, just go to:

https://winkomibooks.com/opt-in-page-Khaula

Inside the books, you will discover:

- A special bold & easy coloring book perfect for relaxing after practice
- A Silly Sentence Handwriting game perfect for family fun
- Unlimited Handwriting practice sheets

If you want to have more fun and get even better at handwriting, make sure to grab the free books.

✦ A Quick Note from the Author

Hi there! 👋

Thank you so much for choosing this handwriting workbook. With so many options out there, I'm truly honored you picked this one.

If you and your child enjoy the book, I'd be so grateful if you could leave a quick review on Amazon. 📝 ⭐ It really helps other parents and educators discover this resource, and it supports independent authors like me in creating more fun and educational content 🤍.

With gratitude,
Khaula Mubasher

To Leave a Review in US Marketplace, Use the Link or QR Code Below

https://amazon.com/review/create-review/?&asin=B0F5CKMW4K

To Leave a Review in All Other Marketplaces, Use This Link or QR Code

https://mybook.to/JFcYj

© Copyright 2025 Khaula Mubasher – All rights reserved.

No part of this publication may be reproduced, stored in a retrieval system, or transmitted in any form or by any means without the prior written permission of the publisher, except for brief quotations used in reviews.

This book Belongs to

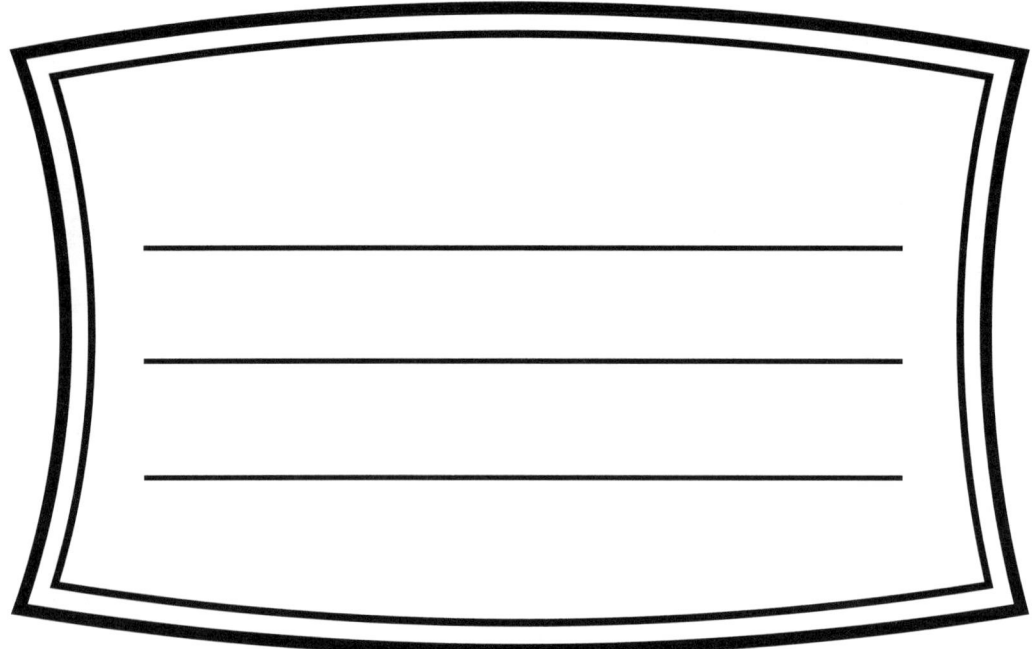

Table of Contents

01   Alphabets
27   Science Facts
78   Jokes and Riddles
130   Mission: Super Shopper
131   Writing a Thank-You Note
133   Writing a Birthday Card
134   Application to be Anything You Want
136   Superhero Application
139   Scientist Profiles

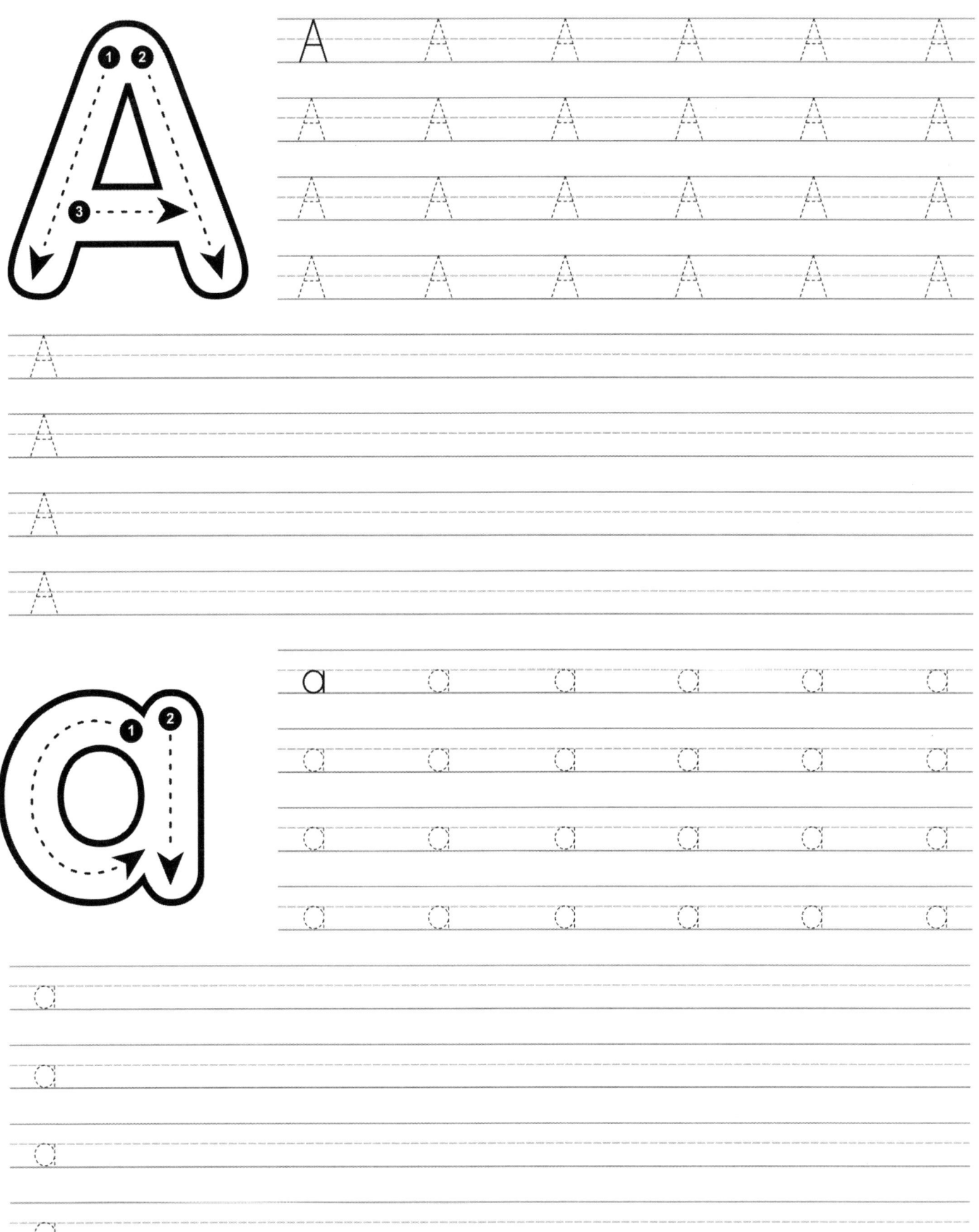

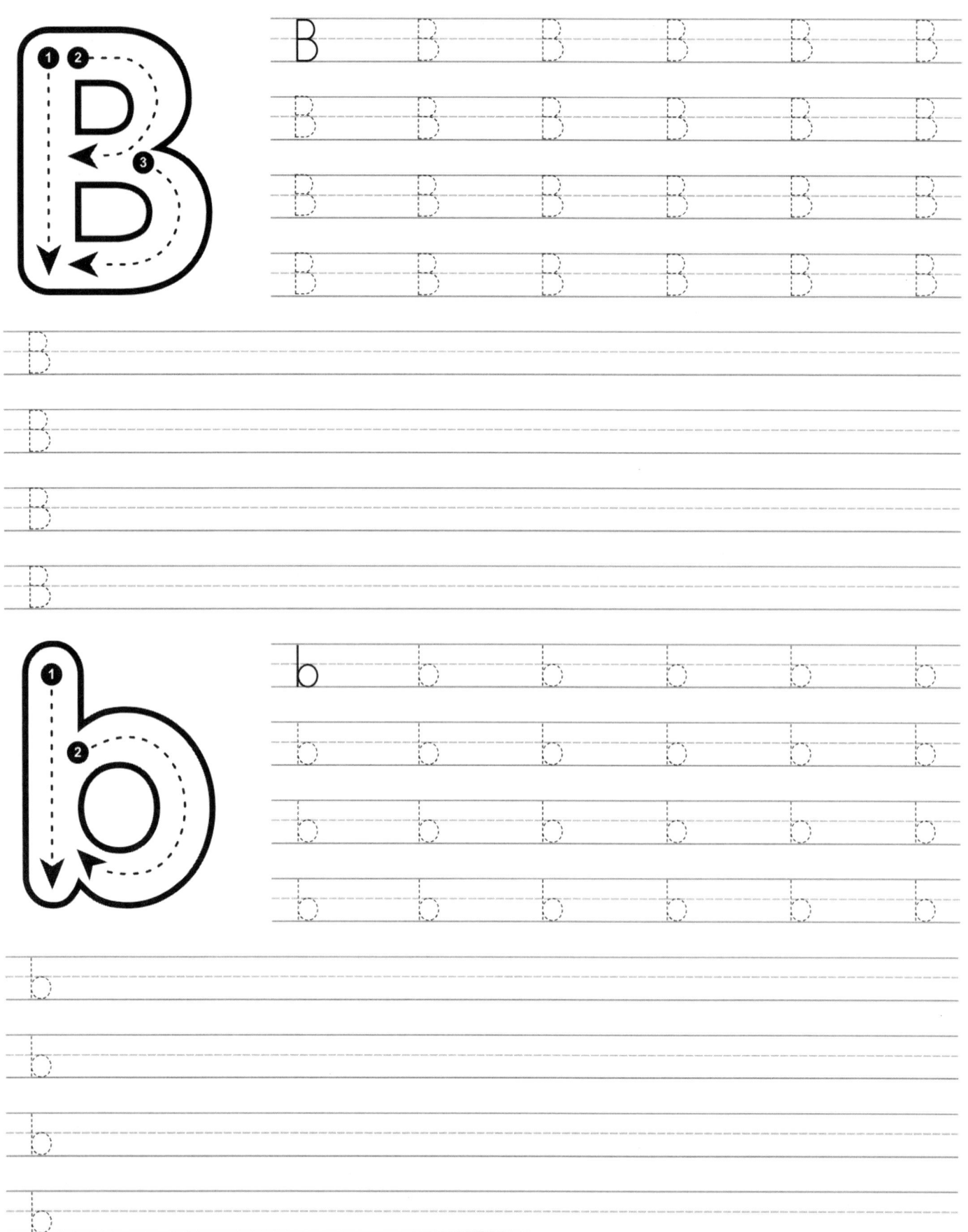

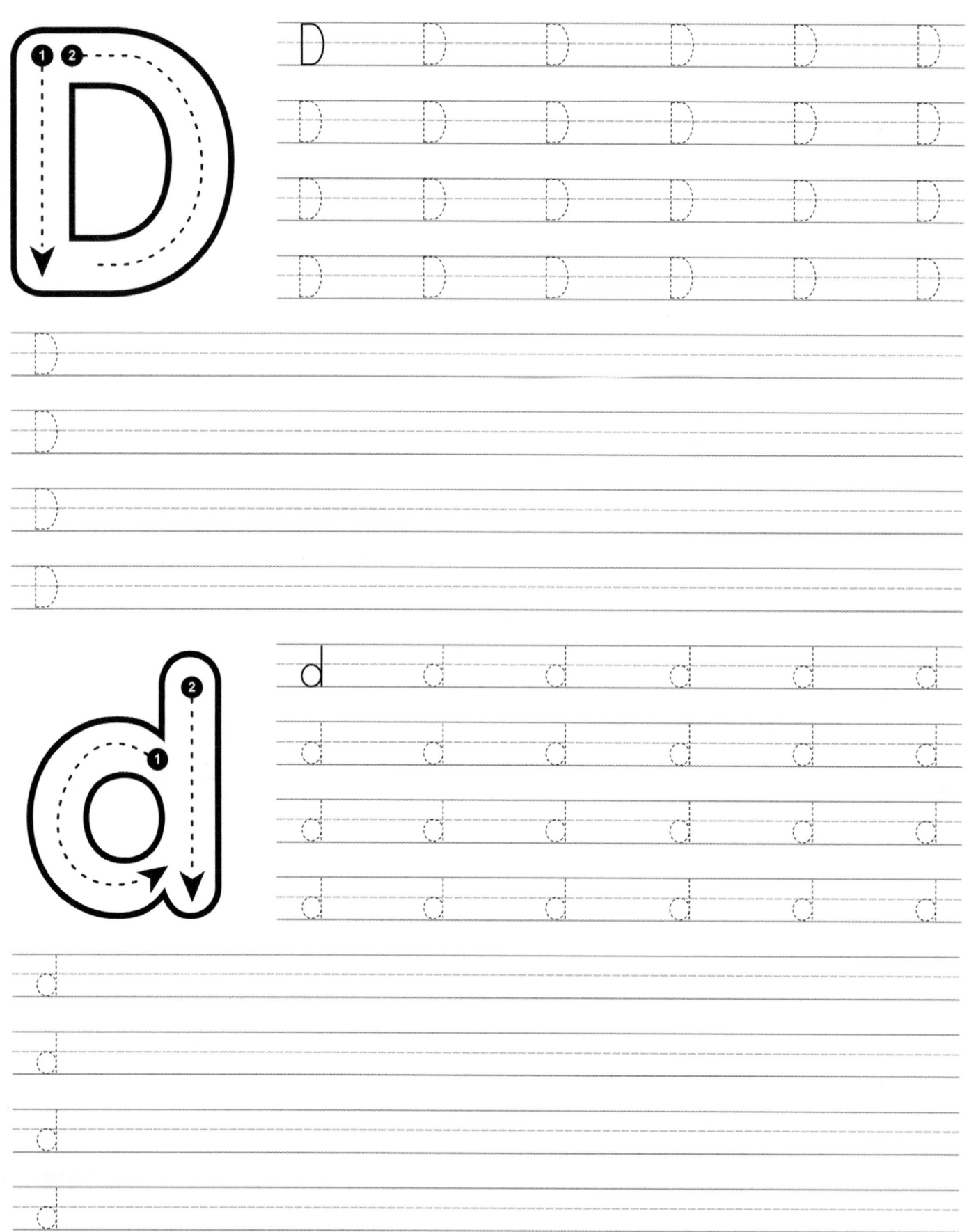

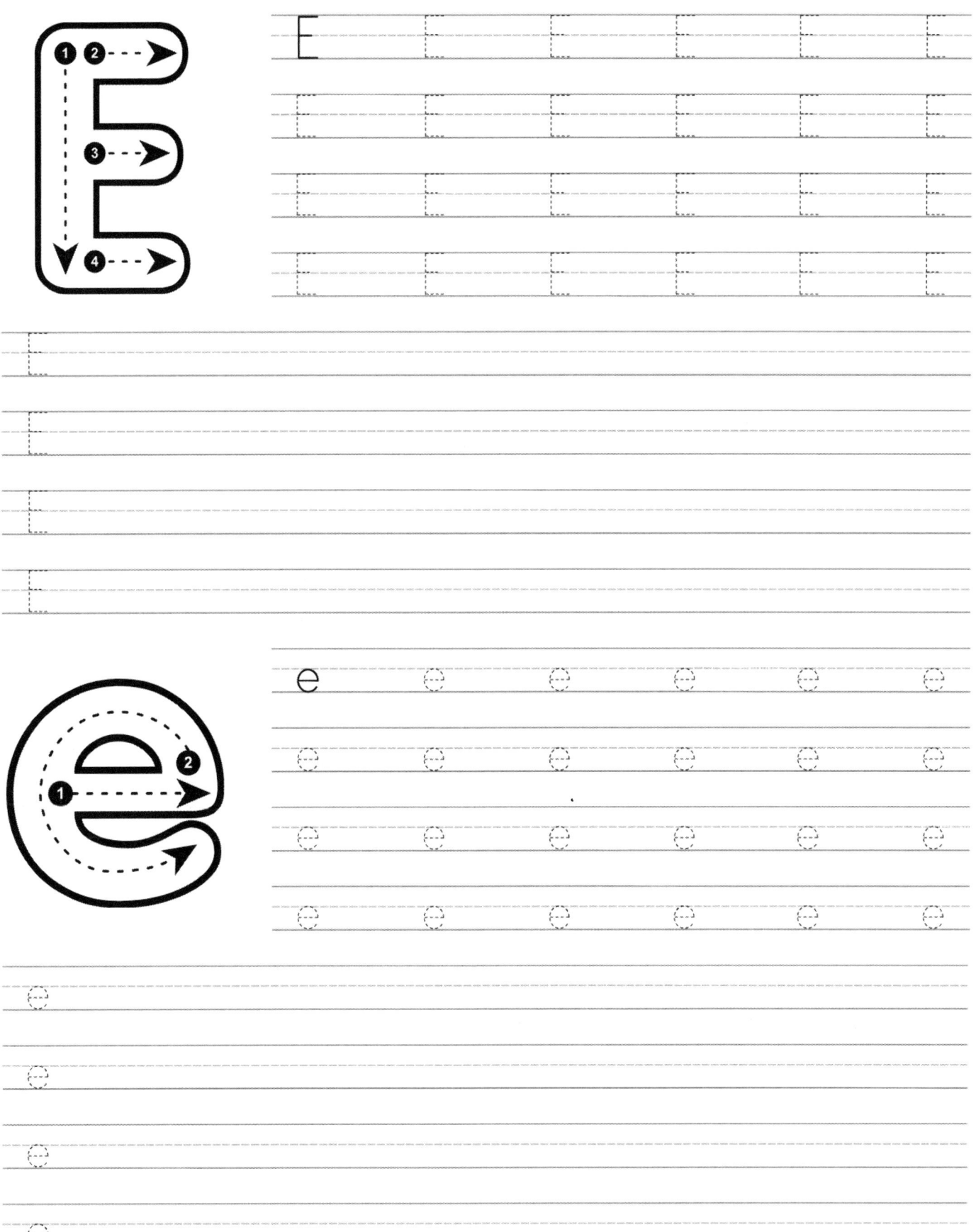

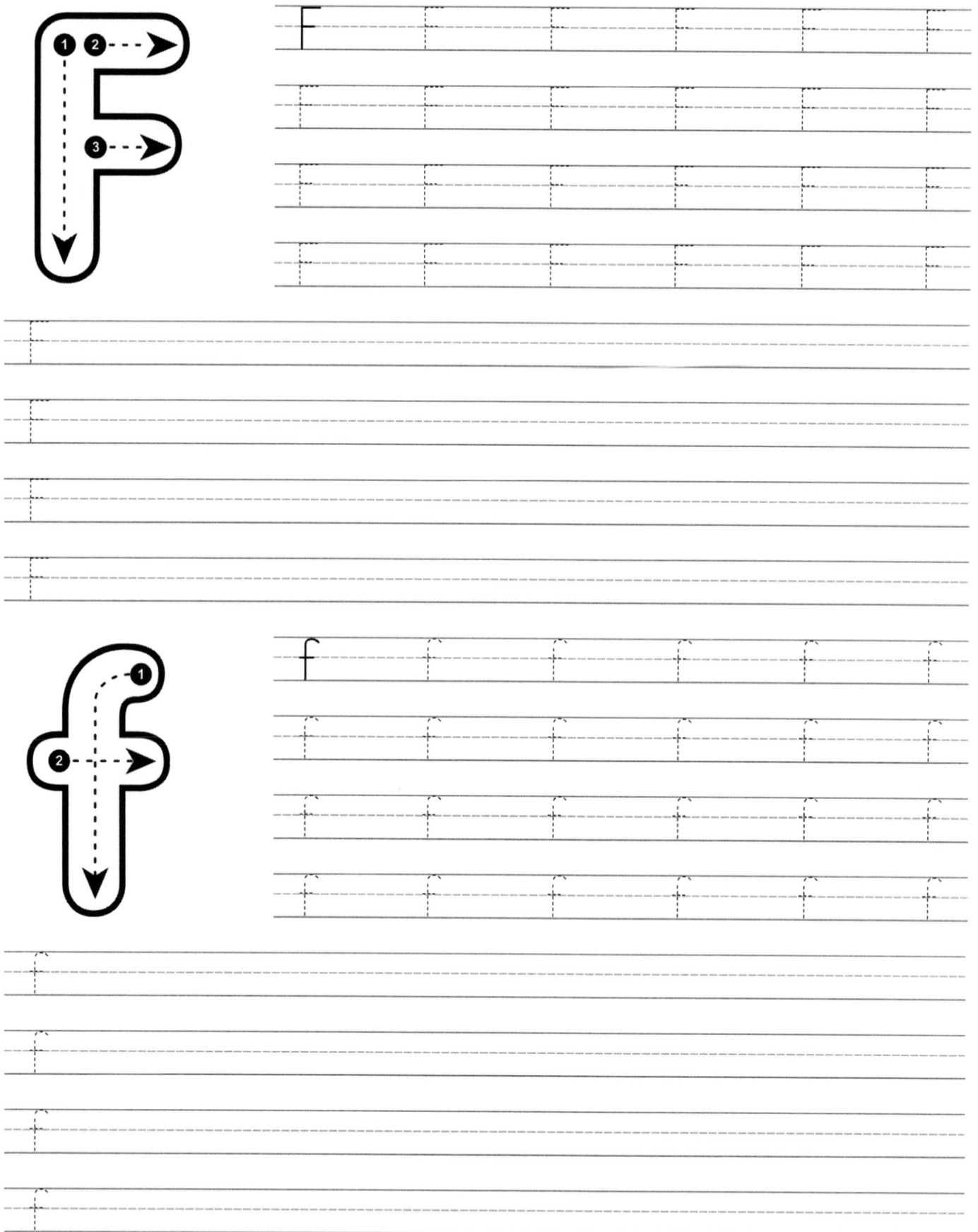

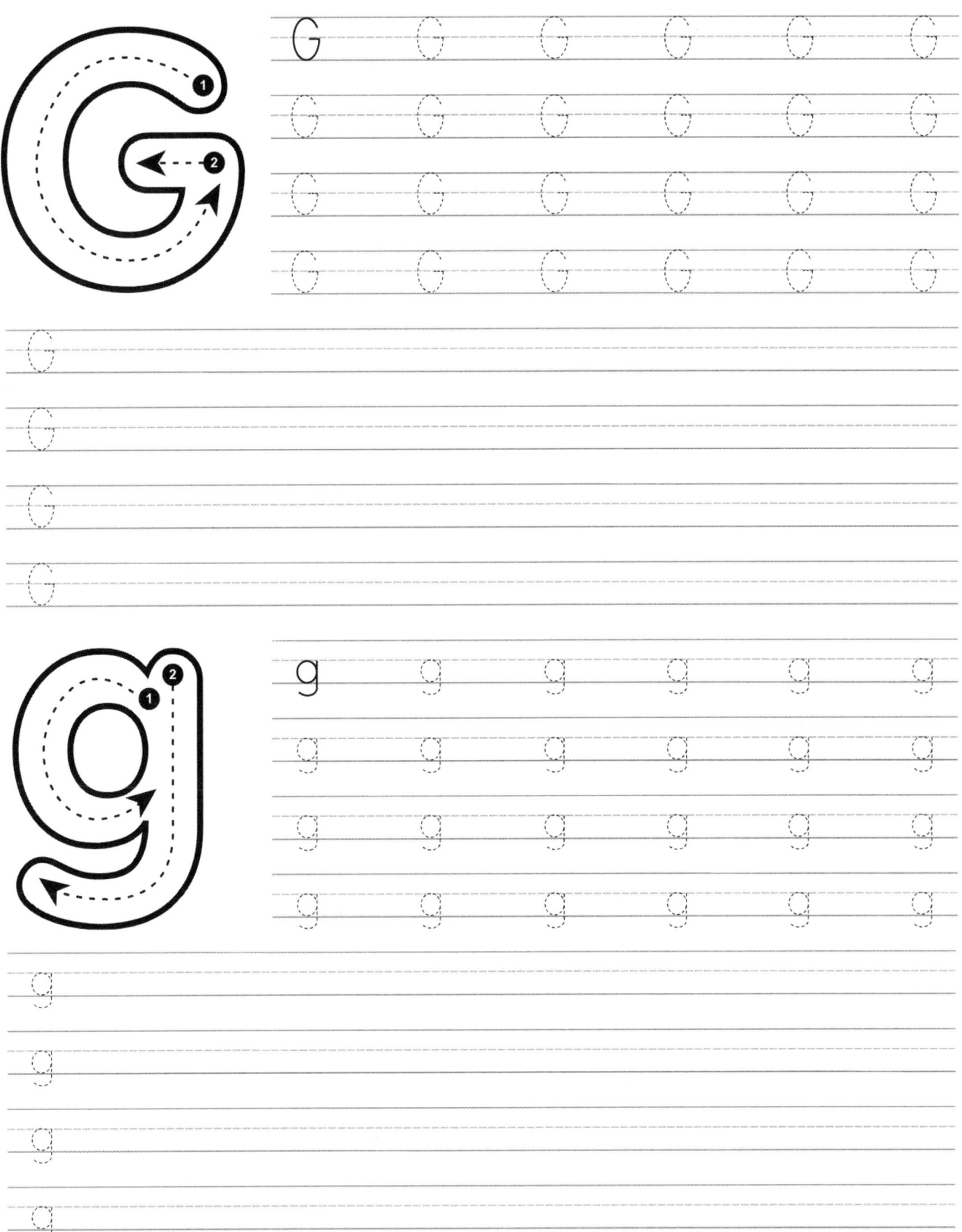

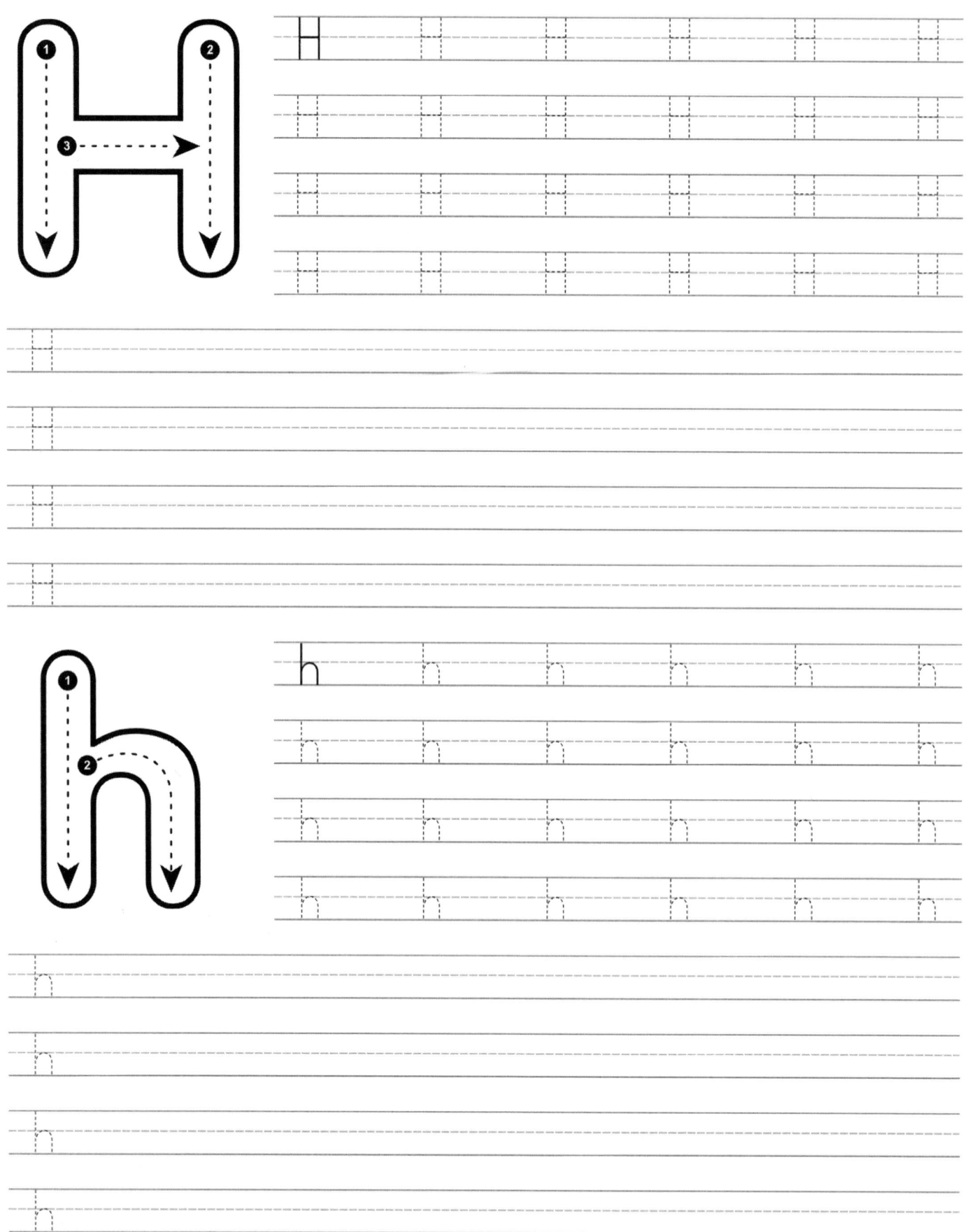

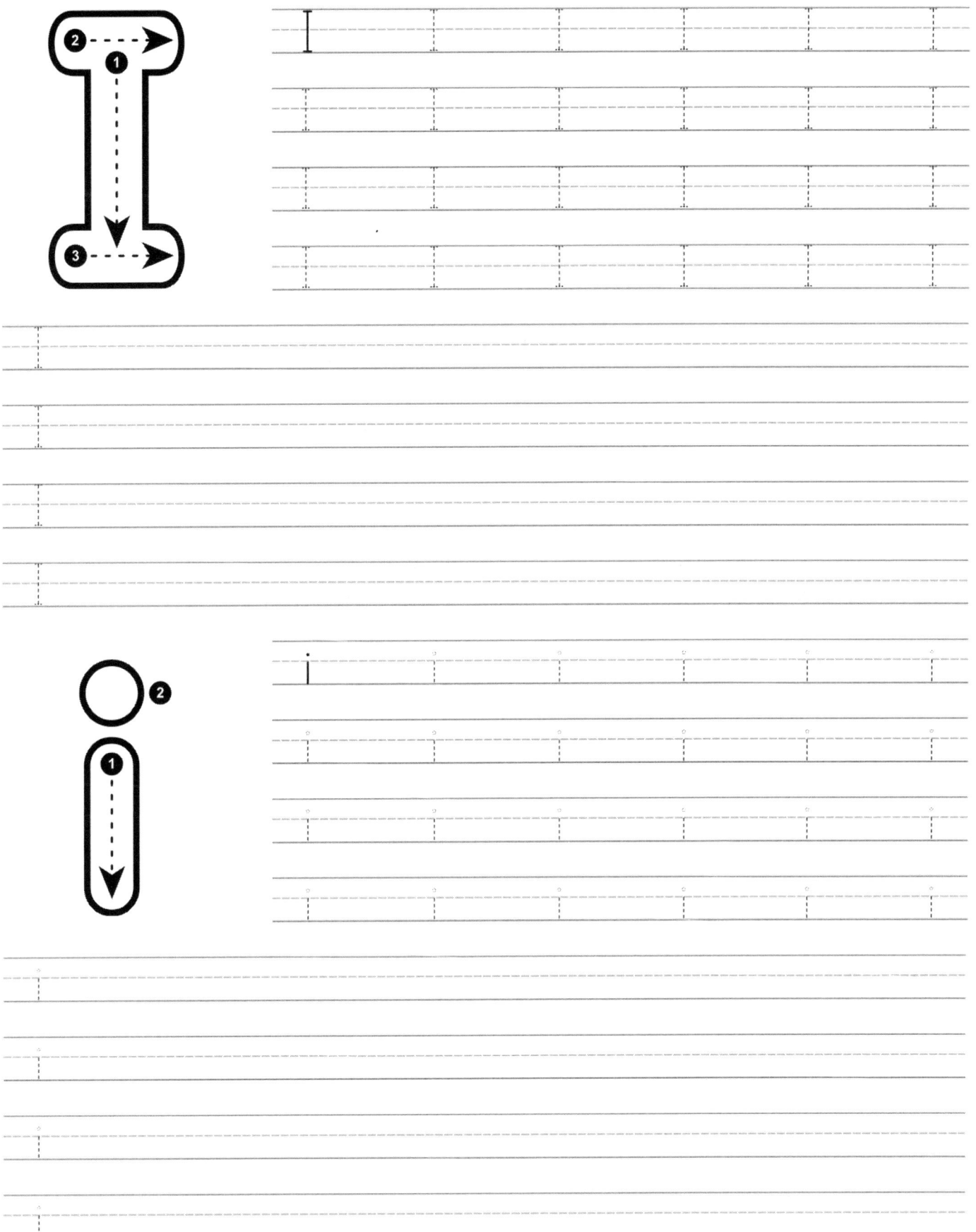

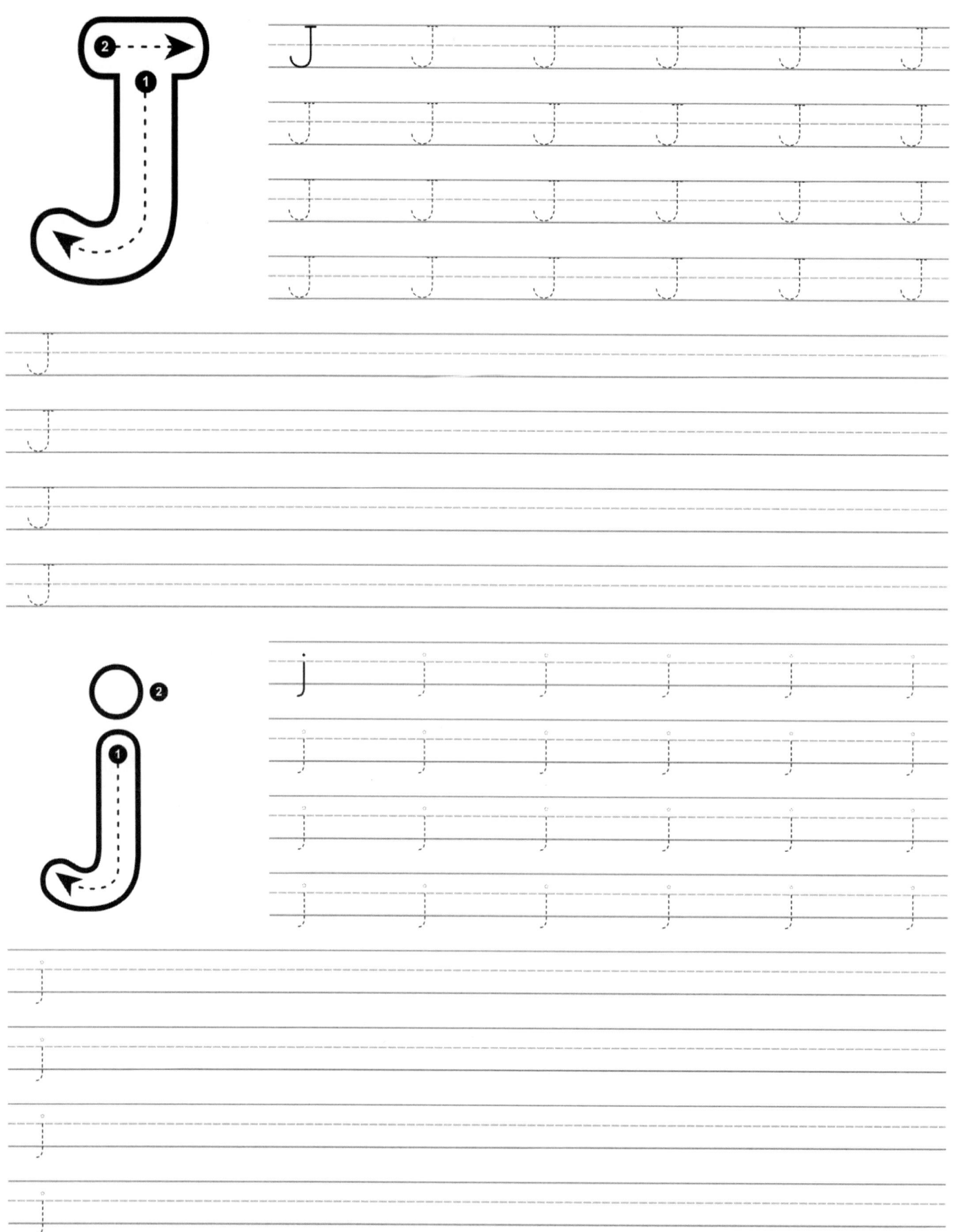

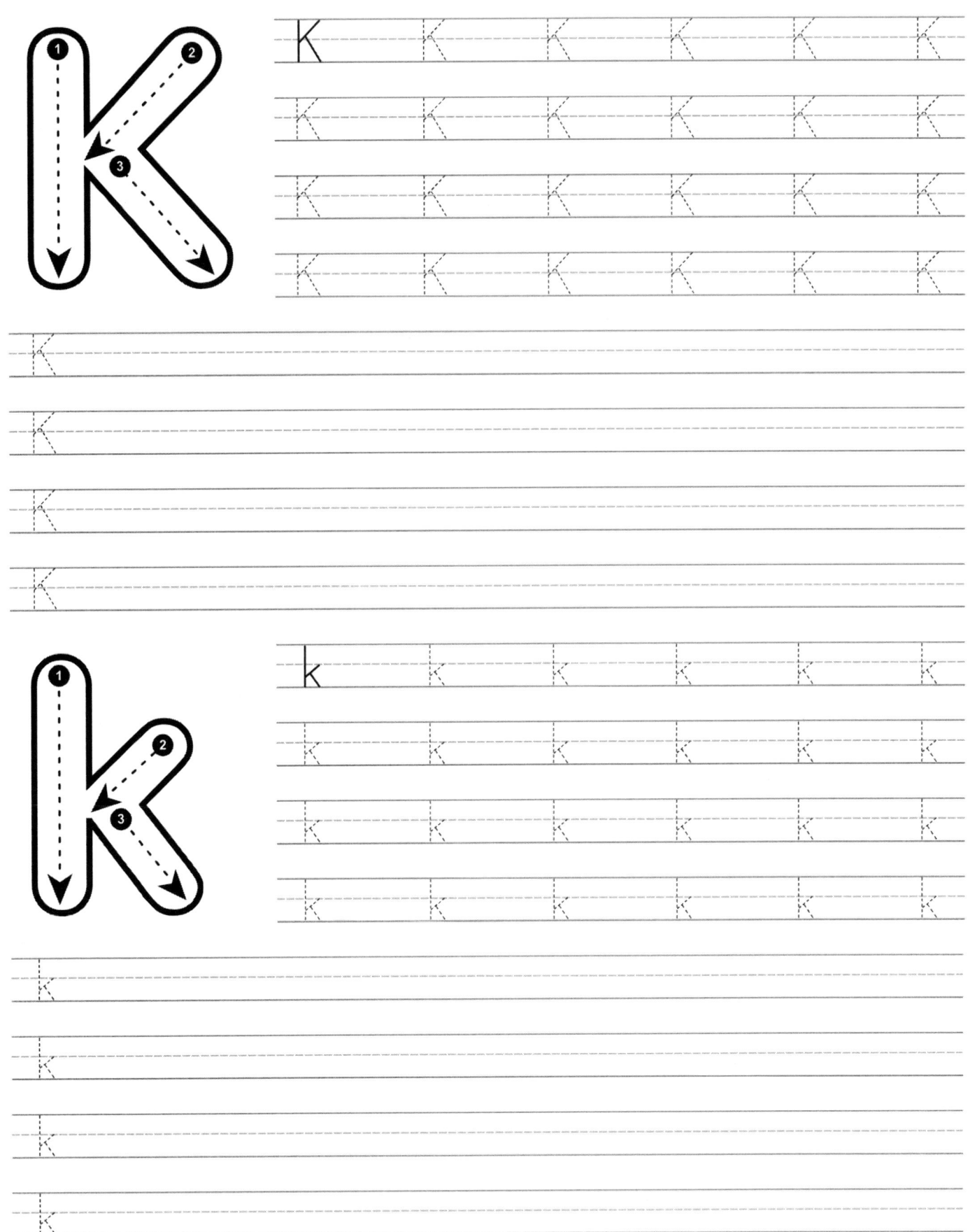

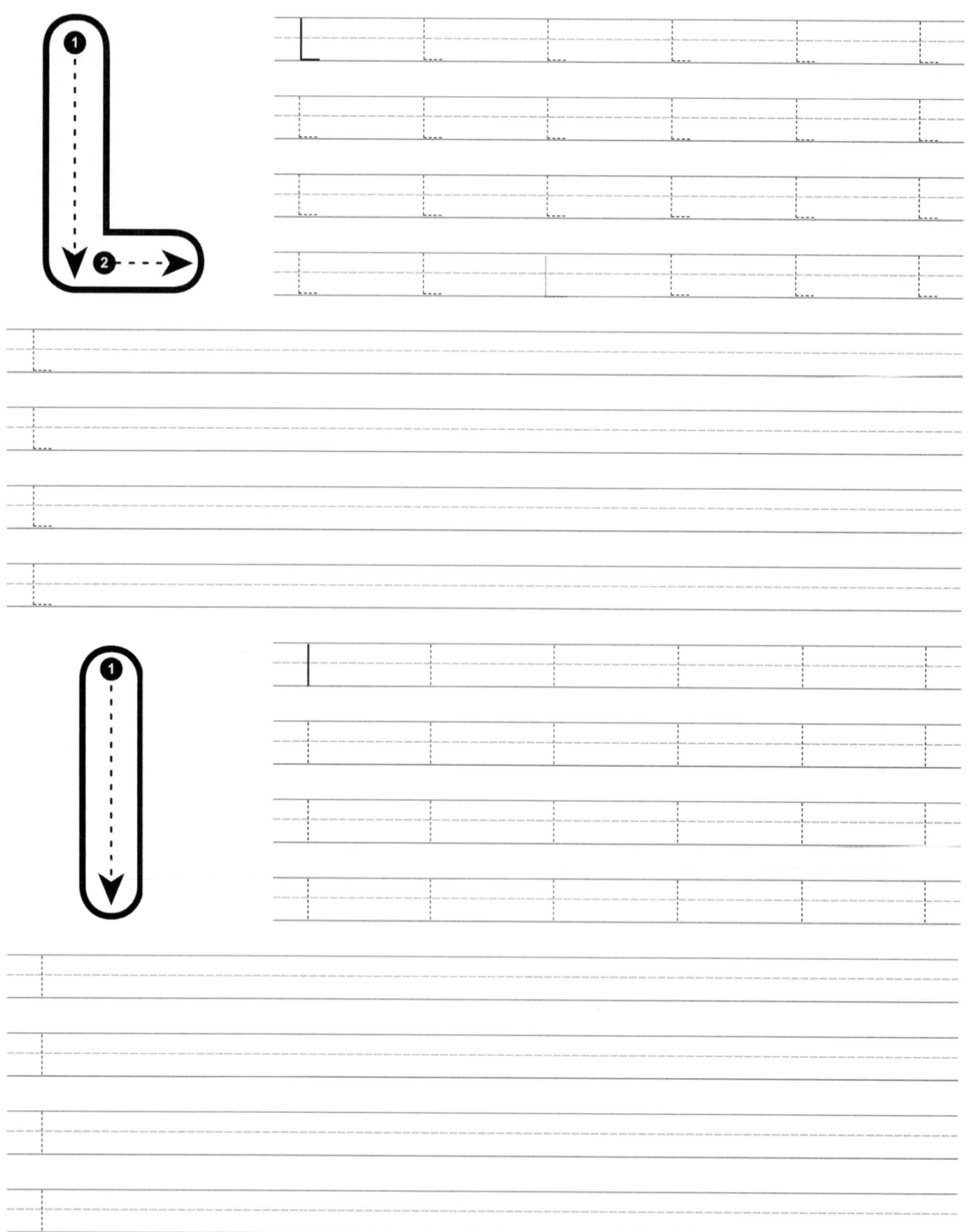

M M M M M M
M M M M M M
M M M M M M
M M M M M M

M
M
M
M

m m m m m m
m m m m m m
m m m m m m
m m m m m m

m
m
m
m

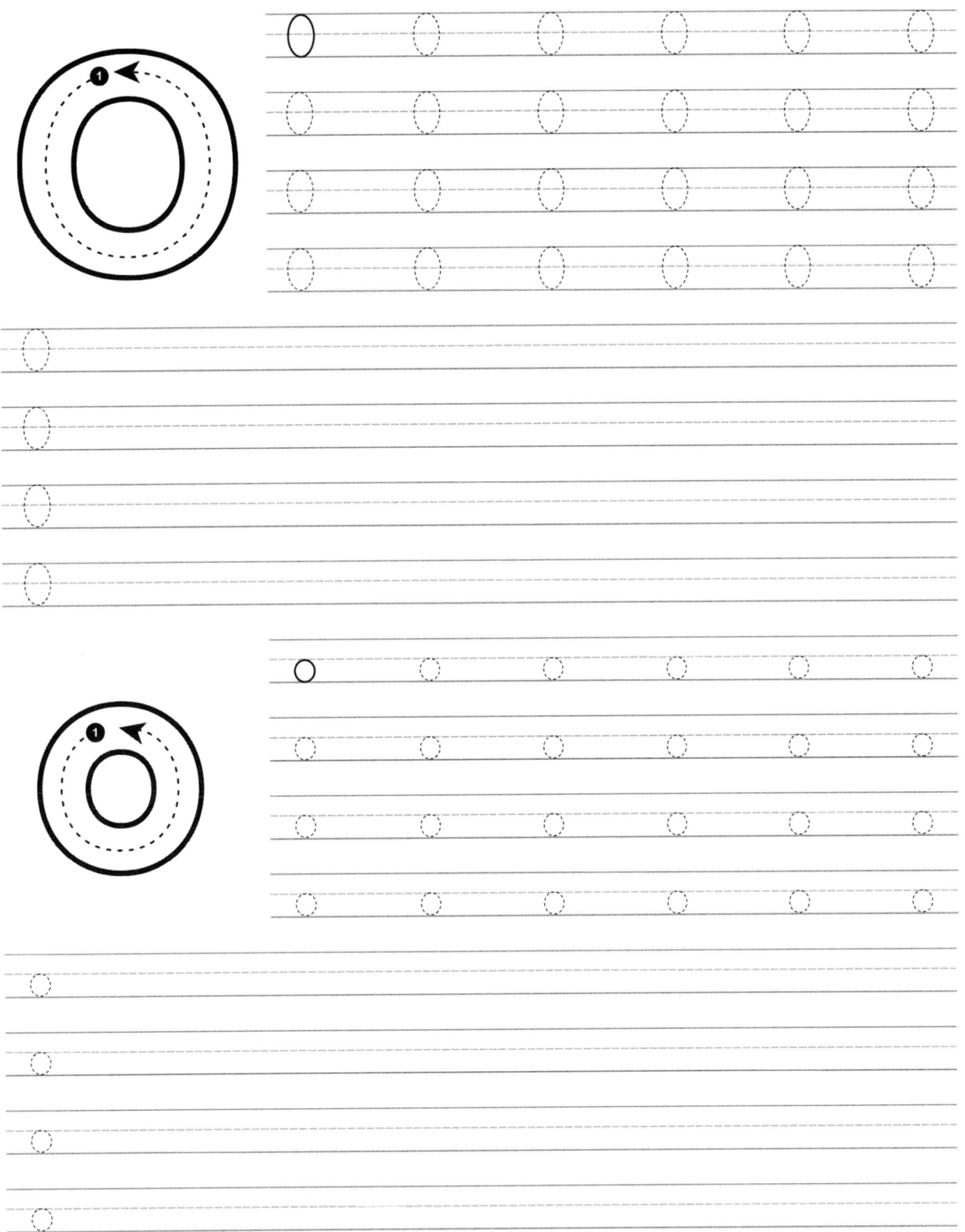

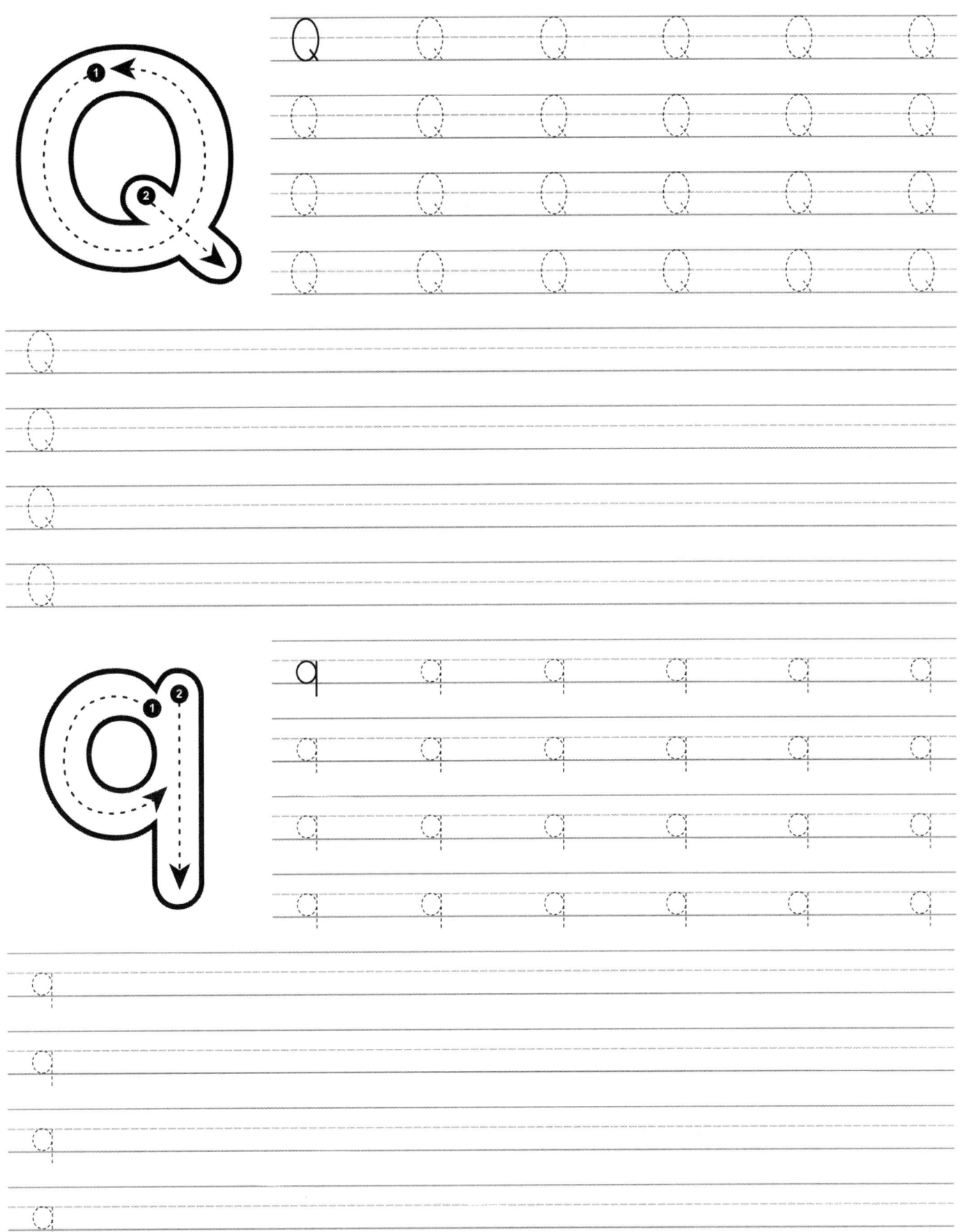

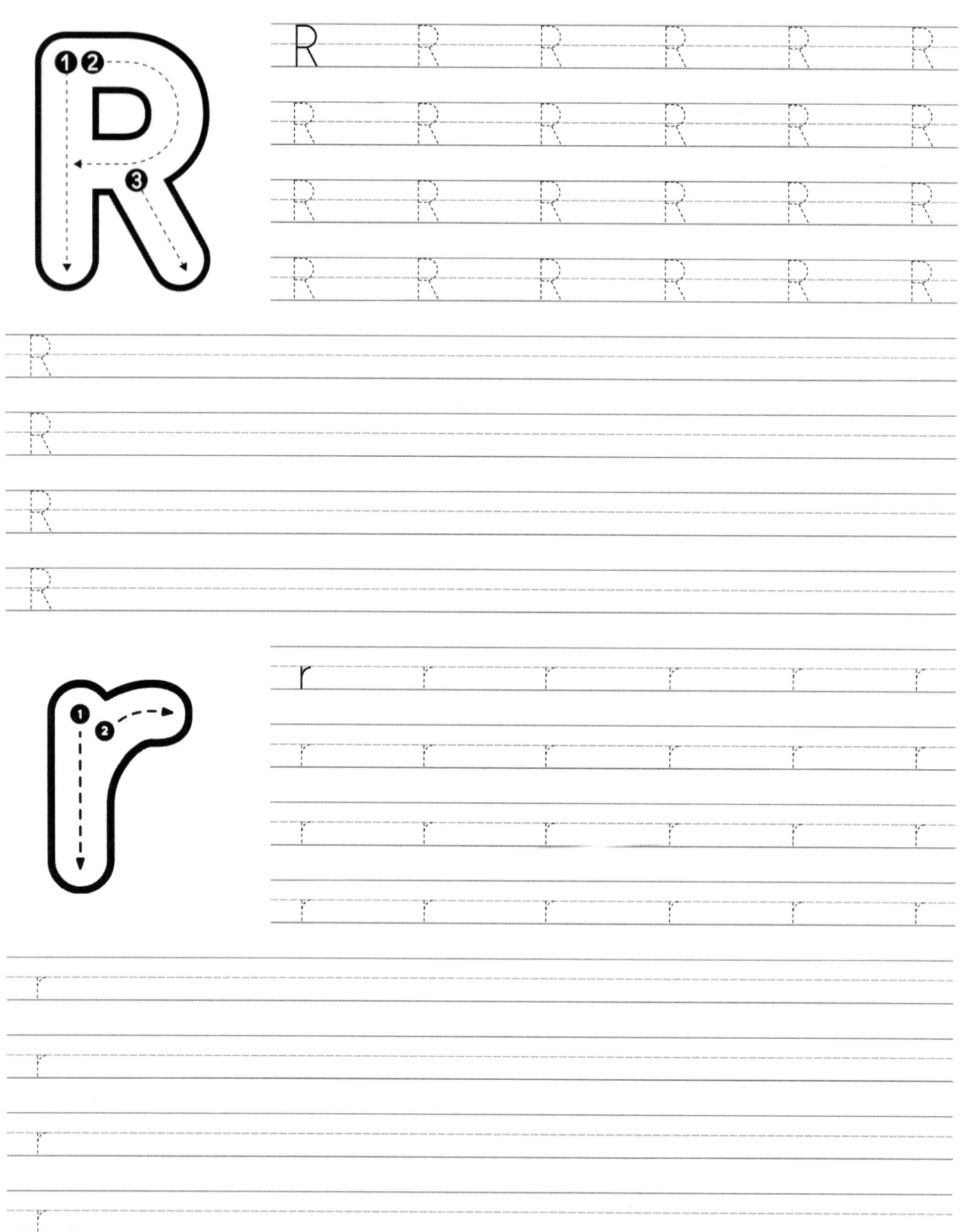

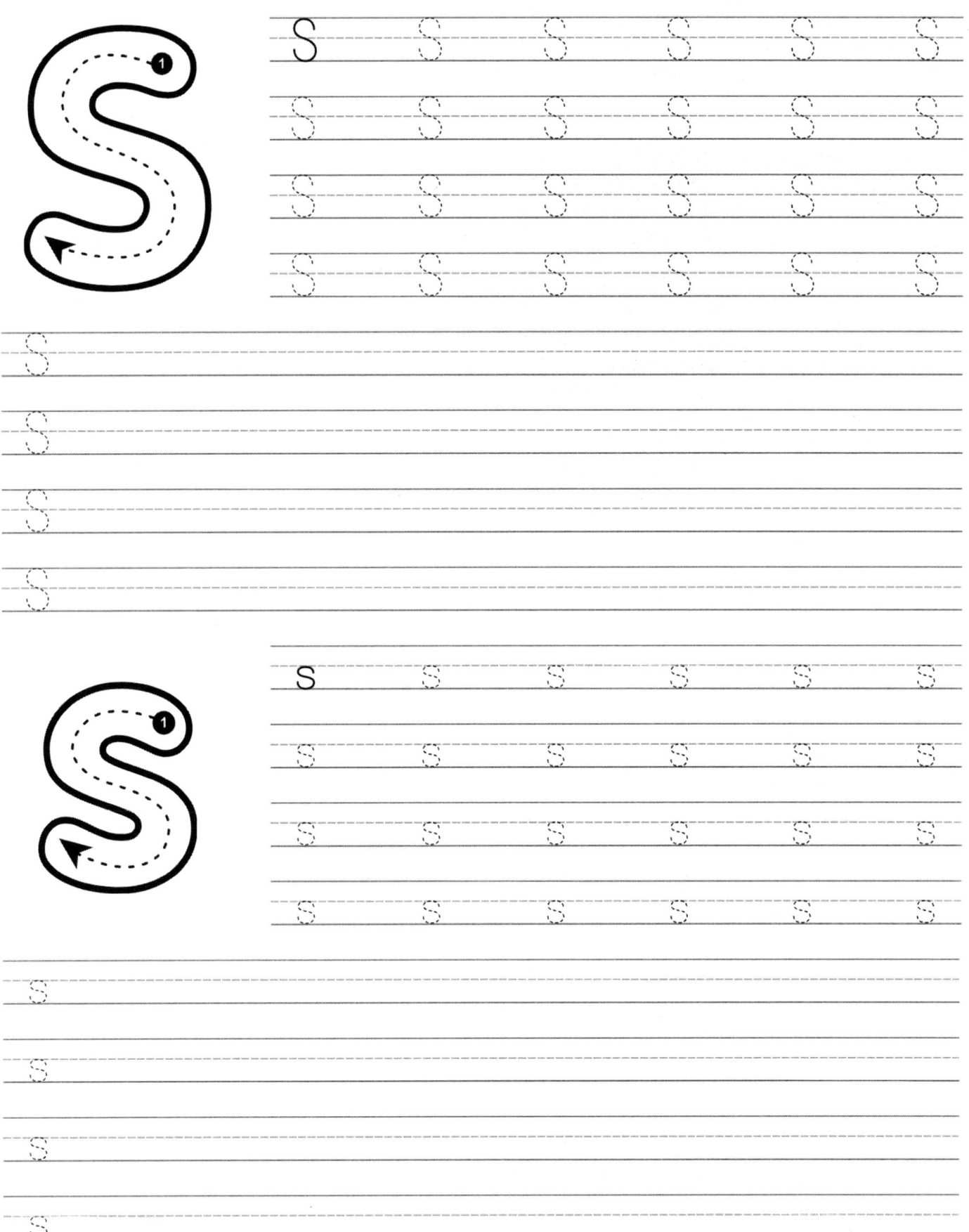

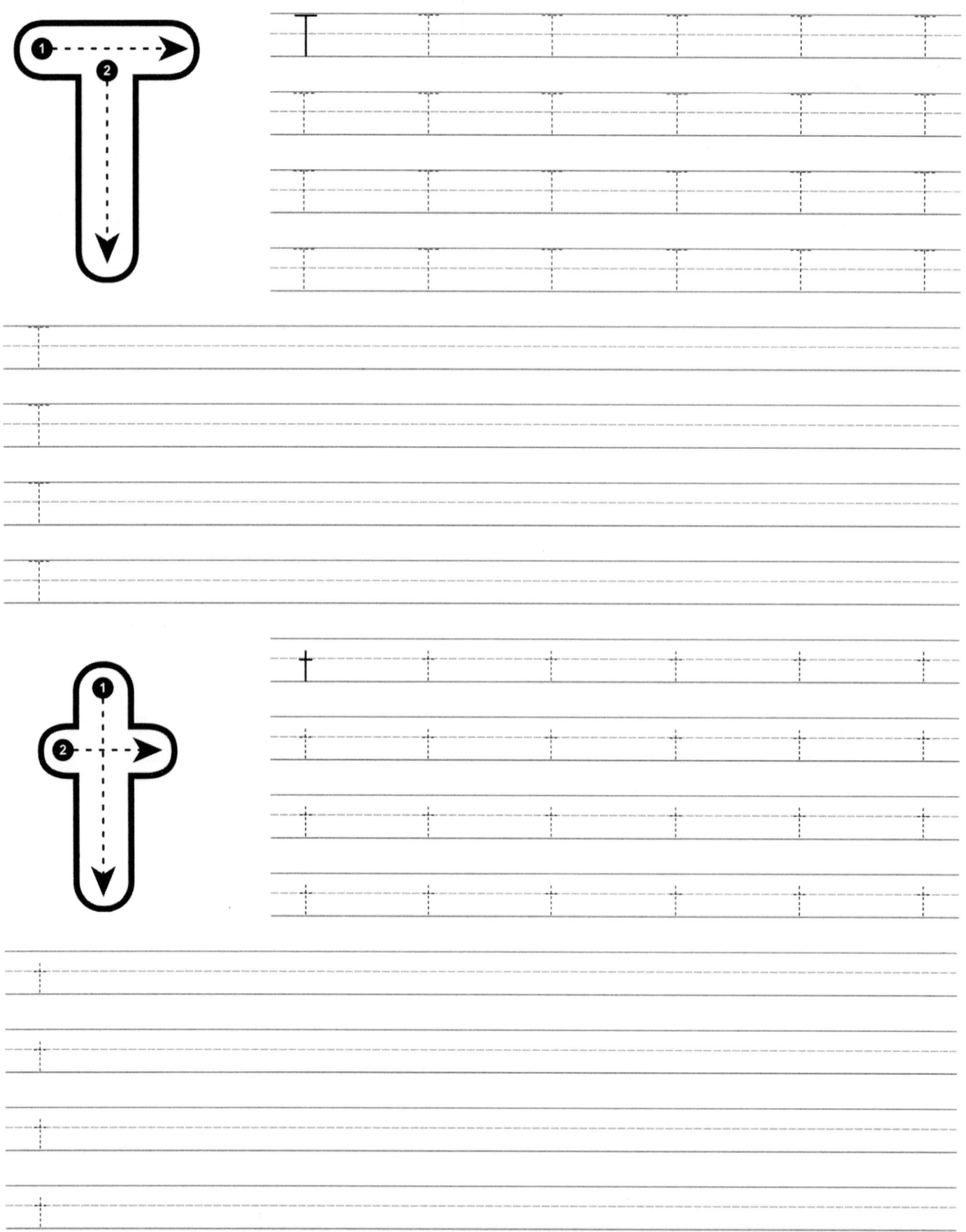

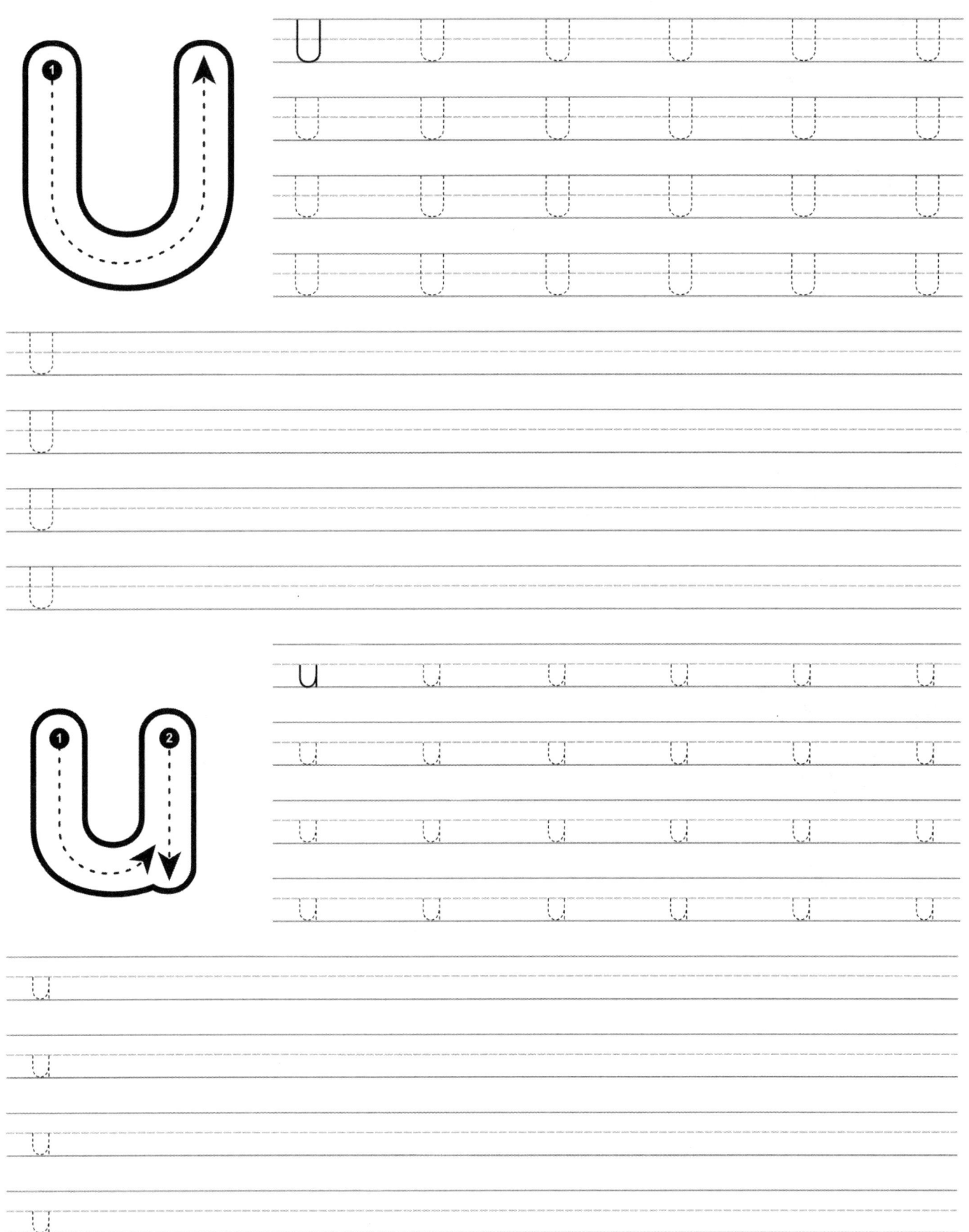

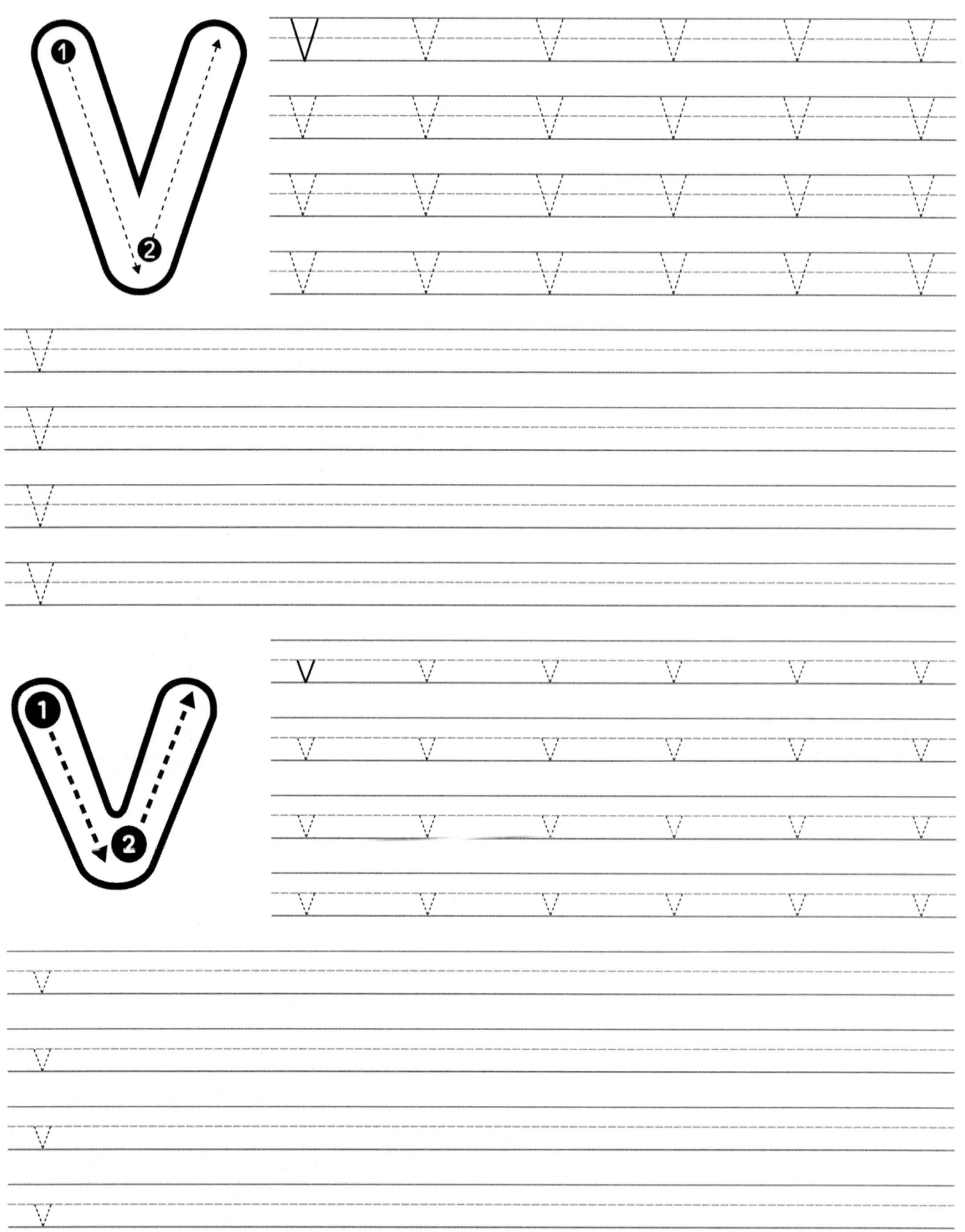

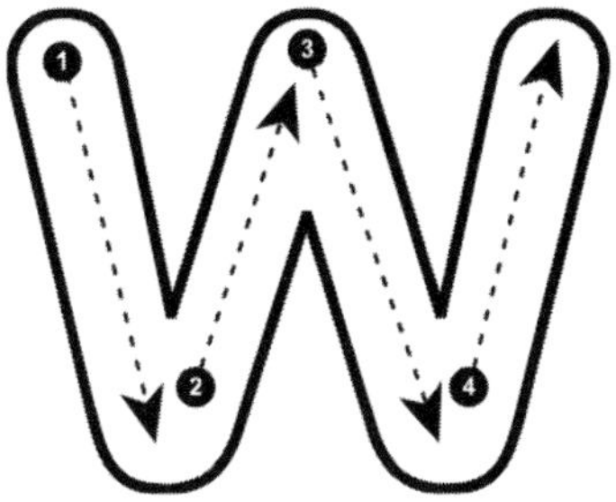

W

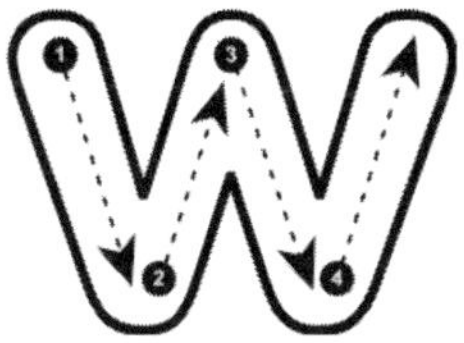

w

25

Science Facts

Mercury's year is just 88 days long!

It zooms around the Sun super fast!

Mercury's year is just 88 days long!

It zooms around the Sun super fast!

Venus spins backward! The Sun rises in

the west and sets in the east!

Venus spins backward! The Sun rises in

the west and sets in the east!

A shrimp's heart is in its head!
Talk about thinking with your heart!

A shrimp's heart is in its head!
Talk about thinking with your heart!

Cows have best friends! They get sad
when separated from their buddies

Cows have best friends! They get sad
when separated from their buddies

A group of flamingos is a flamboyance,
a fancy name for fancy birds!

A group of flamingos is a flamboyance,
a fancy name for fancy birds!

Cheetahs are super fast! They go from
0 to 60 mph in just 3 seconds!

Cheetahs are super fast! They go from
0 to 60 mph in just 3 seconds!

Tigers have striped skin! Even without fur, their stripes stay!

Jellyfish have no brain, heart, or bones! Yet, they've survived millions of years!

Some frogs freeze solid in winter! They thaw out in spring and hop away!

Some frogs freeze solid in winter! They thaw out in spring and hop away!

A chameleon's tongue is super long! It's twice the size of its body!

A chameleon's tongue is super long! It's twice the size of its body!

Hummingbirds can fly backward! They zip around like tiny helicopters!

Hummingbirds can fly backward! They zip around like tiny helicopters!

There's a planet out there—55 Cancri e, that might be made of diamonds!

There's a planet out there—55 Cancri e, that might be made of diamonds!

Your body has iron for a small nail!
It helps blood carry oxygen!

You can't breathe and swallow together!
Your body won't let you!

Your stomach gets a new lining every few days—or it'd digest itself!

Ears never stop growing! They keep getting bigger as you age!

Your brain is 73% water!

That's almost like a watermelon!

Your brain is 73% water!

That's almost like a watermelon!

Your tongue has 8,000 taste buds!

Each one helps detect flavors!

Your tongue has 8,000 taste buds!

Each one helps detect flavors!

Your heart beats 100,000 times daily!
That's 35 million beats every year!
Your heart beats 100,000 times daily!
That's 35 million beats every year!

Stomach acid can dissolve metal! Good
thing your stomach lining protects you!
Stomach acid can dissolve metal! Good
thing your stomach lining protects you!

Water can boil and freeze together!
It happens at the "triple point"!

Some metals explodes in water! Sodium metal bursts into flames when wet!

Lightning is hotter than the Sun!
That's why it glows so brightly!

Lightning is hotter than the Sun!
That's why it glows so brightly!

Saliva helps you taste food! Without
spit, flavors wouldn't be as strong!

Saliva helps you taste food! Without
spit, flavors wouldn't be as strong!

On Uranus, a day flies by in 17 hours, but seasons drag on for 42 years!

On Uranus, a day flies by in 17 hours, but seasons drag on for 42 years!

One million Earths fit inside the Sun! The Sun is HUGE!

One million Earths fit inside the Sun! The Sun is HUGE!

The Amazon makes 20% of our oxygen, no wonder it's called Earth's lungs!

The Amazon makes 20% of our oxygen, no wonder it's called Earth's lungs!

The Sahara was a jungle! Thousands of years ago, it had lakes and trees!

The Sahara was a jungle! Thousands of years ago, it had lakes and trees!

It rains diamonds on Neptune! Super
high pressure turns carbon into gems!

It rains diamonds on Neptune! Super
high pressure turns carbon into gems!

Mount Everest grows taller yearly!
Tectonic plates push it up 4 millimeters!

Mount Everest grows taller yearly!
Tectonic plates push it up 4 millimeters!

Trees "talk" through roots! They send warning signals to each other!

Trees "talk" through roots! They send warning signals to each other!

Earth spins at 1,000 mph! But we don't feel it!

Earth spins at 1,000 mph! But we don't feel it!

Tyrannosaurus had the strongest bite!
Enough to crush a car!

Tyrannosaurus had the strongest bite!
Enough to crush a car!

Some dinosaurs had feathers!
Velociraptors looked like giant birds!

Some dinosaurs had feathers!
Velociraptors looked like giant birds!

The biggest dino was 120 feet long!
Argentinosaurus was HUGE!

The biggest dino was 120 feet long!
Argentinosaurus was HUGE!

Dinosaurs ruled for 165 million years!
Way longer than humans!

Dinosaurs ruled for 165 million years!
Way longer than humans!

"Dinosaur" means "terrible lizard"!
Named in 1842!

"Dinosaur" means "terrible lizard"!
Named in 1842!

Triceratops had 800 teeth! They kept growing new ones!

Triceratops had 800 teeth! They kept growing new ones!

Some dinosaurs were chicken-sized!

Microraptor was tiny and could glide!

Spinosaurus was bigger than

Tyrannosaurus and it loved water!

The Eiffel Tower grows in summer!
Heat makes metal expand!

The Eiffel Tower grows in summer!
Heat makes metal expand!

Planes fly because of curved wings!
They create lift!

Planes fly because of curved wings!
They create lift!

The internet started in 1983!

It began as a military project!

The internet started in 1983!

It began as a military project!

3D printers can make food!

Even pizzas and chocolate!

3D printers can make food!

Even pizzas and chocolate!

Some robots do surgery! Super precise movements help doctors!

Some robots do surgery! Super precise movements help doctors!

Velcro came from plant burrs! Inspired by nature!

Velcro came from plant burrs! Inspired by nature!

The first computer was room-sized!
ENIAC took up 1,800 square feet!

The first computer was room-sized!
ENIAC took up 1,800 square feet!

The first car was built in 1885! It had
three wheels and could go only 10 mph!

The first car was built in 1885! It had
three wheels and could go only 10 mph!

Coca-Cola was originally green—before they added the current color!

Apples float because they are 25% air! That's why bobbing for apples works!

Carrots were originally purple!

Orange ones became popular later!

Carrots were originally purple!

Orange ones became popular later!

A potato can power a battery! It has electrolytes that conduct electricity!

A potato can power a battery! It has electrolytes that conduct electricity!

Chocolate was once money! Aztecs used cocoa beans for trading!

Chocolate was once money! Aztecs used cocoa beans for trading!

Bananas are slightly radioactive! They have potassium-40, but it's safe to eat!

Bananas are slightly radioactive! They have potassium-40, but it's safe to eat!

Liquid nitrogen makes instant ice cream!
It freezes the mix super fast!

Liquid nitrogen makes instant ice cream!
It freezes the mix super fast!

Driving to the Moon? At highway speed,
it'd take six months!

Driving to the Moon? At highway speed,
it'd take six months!

Water expands when it freezes!
That's why ice floats instead of sinking!

Water expands when it freezes!
That's why ice floats instead of sinking!

Your eyes can see 10 million colors!
That's a rainbow of possibilities!

Your eyes can see 10 million colors!
That's a rainbow of possibilities!

There's a metal that melts in your hand!
Gallium melts at just 85°F (29°C)!

There's a metal that melts in your hand!
Gallium melts at just 85°F (29°C)!

The ocean holds 20 million tons of gold!
But it's too spread out to collect!

The ocean holds 20 million tons of gold!
But it's too spread out to collect!

A spoonful of black hole is heavy! It weighs as much as a whole mountain!

A spoonful of black hole is heavy! It weighs as much as a whole mountain!

Saturn's rings are mostly ice! Some pieces are tiny, others as big as houses!

Saturn's rings are mostly ice! Some pieces are tiny, others as big as houses!

Neptune has a giant storm! The "Great
Dark Spot" is bigger than Earth!

Neptune has a giant storm! The "Great
Dark Spot" is bigger than Earth!

Octopuses have three hearts! Two
pump to gills, one pumps to the body!

Octopuses have three hearts! Two
pump to gills, one pumps to the body!

Your skin replaces itself! Every 27 days, you get a new outer layer

Your skin replaces itself! Every 27 days, you get a new outer layer

Bones are five times stronger than steel (pound for pound)

Bones are five times stronger than steel (pound for pound)

Fingernails grow faster! They get more sun and movement than toenails!

Fingernails grow faster! They get more sun and movement than toenails!

Glass moves super slowly! Old windows get thicker at the bottom over time!

Glass moves super slowly! Old windows get thicker at the bottom over time!

Earth's driest place! The Atacama
Desert hasn't had rain in 2 million years!

Antarctica holds tons of water! If it
melted, oceans would rise 200 feet!

Dino fossils are everywhere-even
Antarctica!

Dino fossils are everywhere-even
Antarctica!

Microwaves were a happy accident,
a radar melted a scientist's chocolate!

Microwaves were a happy accident,
a radar melted a scientist's chocolate!

A fruit tastes like chocolate! Black sapote has a creamy chocolate flavor!

Honey never spoils! 3,000-year-old honey was found still safe to eat!

Slime is science magic! Mixing glue and borax makes stretchy, rubber-like chains!

Slime is science magic! Mixing glue and borax makes stretchy, rubber-like chains!

Venus is the hottest planet! Thick clouds trap heat, reaching 900°F (475°C)!

Venus is the hottest planet! Thick clouds trap heat, reaching 900°F (475°C)!

Earth is mostly water! Oceans cover 71%, so it's called the "Blue Planet"!

Earth is mostly water! Oceans cover 71%, so it's called the "Blue Planet"!

Some mushrooms glow! They make light, like nature's nightlights!

Some mushrooms glow! They make light, like nature's nightlights!

Sharks are older than trees—swimming for 400 million years!

Sharks are older than trees—swimming for 400 million years!

Astronauts grow taller in space! Without gravity, they stretch about 2 inches!

Astronauts grow taller in space! Without gravity, they stretch about 2 inches!

Fire can't burn in space! It needs oxygen, but there's none up there!

Fire can't burn in space! It needs oxygen, but there's none up there!

One day on Venus takes 243 Earth days! That's longer than its entire year!

One day on Venus takes 243 Earth days! That's longer than its entire year!

Octopuses change color! They blend in or show feelings with special skin cells!

Octopuses change color! They blend in or show feelings with special skin cells!

You cannot burp in space! Gravity keeps gas mixed with food in your stomach!

You cannot burp in space! Gravity keeps gas mixed with food in your stomach!

Moon footprints last forever! No wind or water means they never fade!

Lake Natron turns animals to stone, its salty water preserves them!

Your phone is powerful! It could've helped land astronauts on the Moon!

Earth's core is hotter than the Sun! It reaches 10,800°F (6,000°C)!

Your blood zooms 12,000 miles a day—halfway around the world!

Your blood zooms 12,000 miles a day—halfway around the world!

Wombat poop is cube-shaped! Their intestines shape it to stop rolling away!

Wombat poop is cube-shaped! Their intestines shape it to stop rolling away!

Space smells like burnt steak due to high-energy particles! Strange but true!

Watermelons can explode! Fermentation causes pressure that makes them burst!

A day on Uranus is weird! It rotates on its side, making wild seasons!

A day on Uranus is weird! It rotates on its side, making wild seasons!

Ants never sleep! They take tiny rest breaks but never fully sleep like humans!

Ants never sleep! They take tiny rest breaks but never fully sleep like humans!

Cold air slows sound! Warm air makes it move faster!

Cold air slows sound! Warm air makes it move faster!

A waterfall is underwater! The Denmark Strait has one taller than any on land!

A waterfall is underwater! The Denmark Strait has one taller than any on land!

Bananas are berries! But strawberries aren't, real berries have seeds inside!

Fleas jump like superheroes! They leap 100 times their height!

You share 60% of your DNA with a banana! We're more alike than you think!

You share 60% of your DNA with a banana! We're more alike than you think!

Venus has metal snow! Hot metals turn to gas, then snow down!

Venus has metal snow! Hot metals turn to gas, then snow down!

Jokes

Why was the math book feeling sad?
It had too many unsolved problems!
Why was the math book feeling sad?
It had too many unsolved problems!

What do you call a cow with no legs?
Ground beef!
What do you call a cow with no legs?
Ground beef!

Why did the smartphone go to art school? It wanted to improve its selfies!

Why did the smartphone go to art school? It wanted to improve its selfies!

How does a computer stay cool? It opens all its Windows!

How does a computer stay cool? It opens all its Windows!

How do smart bulbs relax?
They take a light break!
How do smart bulbs relax?
They take a light break!

Why can't you trust tacos?
They always spill the beans!
Why can't you trust tacos?
They always spill the beans!

What did the spoon say to the soup?
I've been stirring things up!

What did the spoon say to the soup?
I've been stirring things up!

How do raindrops greet each other?
They make a splash!

How do raindrops greet each other?
They make a splash!

Why did the turtle start a business?
It wanted to come out of its shell!
Why did the turtle start a business?
It wanted to come out of its shell!

Why couldn't the door go to the dance?
It was un-hinged!
Why couldn't the door go to the dance?
It was un-hinged!

What did the hamster say when it got a new wheel? This is wheel-y exciting!

What did the hamster say when it got a new wheel? This is wheel-y exciting!

What's a rock's favorite cereal? Fruity Pebbles!

What's a rock's favorite cereal? Fruity Pebbles!

What did one wall say to the other wall?
I'll meet you at the corner!
What did one wall say to the other wall?
I'll meet you at the corner!

Why did the golfer bring an extra pair
of pants? In case he got a hole in one!
Why did the golfer bring an extra pair
of pants? In case he got a hole in one!

What did the Roblox player say when they won a game? Easy dubs, no cap!

What's brown and sticky?
A stick!

Why can't Elsa hold a balloon?
Because she'll let it goooo!

Why can't Elsa hold a balloon?
Because she'll let it goooo!

What's an impostor's favorite snack?
Crewmate kebabs!

What's an impostor's favorite snack?
Crewmate kebabs!

What did the zero say to the eight?
Nice belt!

What did the floss dance say to the dab? You're so 2017, brah!

How do Rainbow Friends celebrate winning? They do the Skibbidi dance!

How do Rainbow Friends celebrate winning? They do the Skibbidi dance!

Why was the Griddy so confident? It knew all the right moves!

Why was the Griddy so confident? It knew all the right moves!

What's a dancer's favorite sandwich?
The griddy cheese!
What's a dancer's favorite sandwich?
The griddy cheese!

Why was the electricity bill so
confused? It couldn't keep current!
Why was the electricity bill so
confused? It couldn't keep current!

What does a cloud wear to a fancy party? Thunderwear!

How do scientists freshen their breath? With experi-mints!

What's a penguin's favorite relative?
Their aunt-arctic!

What's a burger's favorite thing in
math? Addition, of extra toppings!

Why did the apple go out with the fig?
Because it couldn't find a date!

Why did the apple go out with the fig?
Because it couldn't find a date!

Why did the spaghetti go to the doctor?
It was feeling strained!

Why did the spaghetti go to the doctor?
It was feeling strained!

What did the salad say to the fridge?
Close the door, I'm dressing!

What did the salad say to the fridge?
Close the door, I'm dressing!

What's full of holes but still holds water? A sponge!

What's full of holes but still holds water? A sponge!

What has wheels and flies but isn't an airplane? A garbage truck!

What has wheels and flies but isn't an airplane? A garbage truck!

What has a head and a tail but no body? A coin!

What has a head and a tail but no body? A coin!

What has a face but can't see, hands but can't grab? A clock

What has a face but can't see, hands but can't grab? A clock

What can you hold without touching it? Your breath!

What can you hold without touching it? Your breath!

What has keys but no locks, space but no room? A keyboard!

What has one eye but can't see? A needle!

What runs around a yard but never moves? A fence!

What runs around a yard but never moves? A fence!

What has teeth but can't eat? A comb!

What has teeth but can't eat? A comb!

What gets bigger the more you take away? A hole!

What gets bigger the more you take away? A hole!

How does a football stay positive? It focuses on its goals!

How does a football stay positive? It focuses on its goals!

Why did the smartphone need glasses?
It lost all its contacts!
Why did the smartphone need glasses?
It lost all its contacts!

What has a bottom at the top?
Your legs!
What has a bottom at the top?
Your legs!

What building has the most stories?
A library!
What building has the most stories?
A library!

What has banks but no money?
A river!
What has banks but no money?
A river!

What did one potato chip say to the other? You're looking crisp today!

Why was the chess piece so calm? It was thinking several moves ahead!

What's a calendar's favorite fruit?
Dates!

What's a calendar's favorite fruit?
Dates!

How do you fix a broken pizza?
With tomato paste!

How do you fix a broken pizza?
With tomato paste!

What do you call a snack that's always scared? Ice cream!

What do you call a snack that's always scared? Ice cream!

What did the hamburger name its baby? Patty!

What did the hamburger name its baby? Patty!

What did one plate say to the other?

Dinner is on me tonight!

What did one plate say to the other?

Dinner is on me tonight!

Why did the chicken join a band?

It had the drumsticks!

Why did the chicken join a band?

It had the drumsticks!

What do you call a peanut in a space suit? An astronut!

What do you call a peanut in a space suit? An astronut!

What do you call a bear with no ears? B!

What do you call a bear with no ears? B!

What did the owl say when it was confused? Hoo knows?

What did the owl say when it was confused? Hoo knows?

How does a penguin build its house? Igloos it together!

How does a penguin build its house? Igloos it together!

How do you catch a squirrel?
Climb a tree and act like a nut!
How do you catch a squirrel?
Climb a tree and act like a nut!

What did one eye say to the other?
Between you and me, something smells!
What did one eye say to the other?
Between you and me, something smells!

Why don't sharks eat clowns?
They taste funny!
Why don't sharks eat clowns?
They taste funny!

What's a cat's favorite dessert?
Chocolate mouse!
What's a cat's favorite dessert?
Chocolate mouse!

What kind of tree fits in your hand?
A palm tree!
What kind of tree fits in your hand?
A palm tree!

Why was math class so hot?
It had too many degrees!
Why was math class so hot?
It had too many degrees!

Why did the gym close down?
It just didn't work out!
Why did the gym close down?
It just didn't work out!

What room can't be entered?
A mushroom!
What room can't be entered?
A mushroom!

What did the triangle say to the circle?
You're pointless!

What did one hat say to the other?

You stay here, I'll go on ahead!

What did one hat say to the other?

You stay here, I'll go on ahead!

Why was the belt arrested?

It was holding up a pair of pants!

Why was the belt arrested?

It was holding up a pair of pants!

Why don't grapes ever tell secrets?
Because they always whine about it!
Why don't grapes ever tell secrets?
Because they always whine about it!

What do you call a bear that smells?
Un-bear-able
What do you call a bear that smells?
Un-bear-able

What do you call a dog that can sing?
A rock 'n' woof star!
What do you call a dog that can sing?
A rock 'n' woof star!

What did the tree say to the
lumberjack? Leaf me alone!
What did the tree say to the
lumberjack? Leaf me alone!

What do you call a bee that can't make up its mind? A maybe!

What do you call a bee that can't make up its mind? A maybe!

Why don't skeletons fight each other? They don't have the guts.

Why don't skeletons fight each other? They don't have the guts.

What does a snowman eat for breakfast? Frosted Flakes!

What does a snowman eat for breakfast? Frosted Flakes!

What do you call a fake noodle? An impasta!

What do you call a fake noodle? An impasta!

What did the ocean say to the shore?
Nothing, it just waved.
What did the ocean say to the shore?
Nothing, it just waved.

Why did the bicycle fall over?
It was two-tired.
Why did the bicycle fall over?
It was two-tired.

What do you get when you cross a snowman and a vampire? Frostbite.

What do you call cheese that isn't yours? Nacho cheese.

How does a cucumber become a pickle?
It goes through a jarring experience.

How does a cucumber become a pickle?
It goes through a jarring experience.

Why don't oysters share their pearls?
Because they're shellfish.

Why don't oysters share their pearls?
Because they're shellfish.

Why did the music teacher need a ladder? To reach the high notes.

Why did the music teacher need a ladder? To reach the high notes.

What do you call a sleeping bull? A bulldozer.

What do you call a sleeping bull? A bulldozer.

What kind of music do mummies listen to? Wrap music!

What kind of music do mummies listen to? Wrap music!

What do you call a lazy kangaroo? A pouch potato!

What do you call a lazy kangaroo? A pouch potato!

Why did the football team go to the bank? To get their quarterback!

Why did the football team go to the bank? To get their quarterback!

What kind of shoes do frogs wear? Open-toad sandals!

What kind of shoes do frogs wear? Open-toad sandals!

Why did the moon break up with the astronaut? It needed space!

Why did the moon break up with the astronaut? It needed space!

Why don't skeletons like to tell secrets? Because they have no body to trust!

Why don't skeletons like to tell secrets? Because they have no body to trust!

What do you call an owl who does
magic? Hoo-dini!

What do you call an owl who does
magic? Hoo-dini!

Why did the dog sit in the shade?
It didn't want to be a hot dog!

Why did the dog sit in the shade?
It didn't want to be a hot dog!

Why did the doughnut go to therapy?
It had too many holes in its life!

Why did the doughnut go to therapy?
It had too many holes in its life!

What's a tree's least favorite month?
Sep-timber!

What's a tree's least favorite month?
Sep-timber!

Why do ducks make great detectives?
They always quack the case!

Why did the teddy bear say no to
dessert? Because it was stuffed!

Why can't your nose be 12 inches long? Because then it would be a foot!

Why can't your nose be 12 inches long? Because then it would be a foot!

What do you call a dinosaur that is sleeping? A dino-snore!

What do you call a dinosaur that is sleeping? A dino-snore!

Fun Activities

Mission: Super Shopper!

Your mom needs help making a shopping list! Write down 10 things she needs from the store.

Things to Include:

Your favorite snacks,
Healthy fruits and veggies,
Ingredients for a fun recipe,
Something for the family pet,

Now make your own list below!

Example: Apples, Bread, Carrots, Cheese

Writing a Thank-You Note

Someone gave you a great gift! Write them a thank-you note to show your appreciation

Dear _____,

Thank you so much for the _____.

I really love it because _____.

I have been using it to _____.

It made my day extra special!

Thanks again for your kindness. You're the best!

Your friend,

_____ (Your Name)

Now write your own thank-you note

Writing a Birthday Card

It's your best friend's birthday! Write them a fun birthday message inside this card.

Dear _____,

Happy Birthday! I hope you have an amazing day filled with _____ (fun thing, like cake, presents, or games). You're such a great friend because _____.

Wishing you lots of happiness and laughter today! Enjoy your special day!

From,

_____ (Your Name)

Fun "Application Form" - Be Anything You Want!

Apply for Your Dream Job!

Fill out this fun application to be something awesome—like a scientist, astronaut, chef, or even a dragon trainer!

Job Title: _____

Your Name: _____

Why do you want this job?
_____
_____
_____
_____

What skills do you have for this job?

1. _____

2. _____

3. _____

What would your work uniform look like?

What's one cool thing you'd do in this job?

Draw yourself doing this job below!

Superhero Application Form

Apply to Join the League of Amazing Superheroes! Fill out this application to create your very own superhero identity!

Superhero Name: _____

Real Name (Secret Identity): _____
_____

Age: _____

City/Planet You Protect: _____

Superpowers (list at least 3):

1. _____

2. _____

3. _____

What's Your Super Suit Like?

Describe the colors, symbols, or gadgets on your costume:

Who is Your Sidekick? (It can be an
animal, a robot, or a friend!)

What's Your Greatest Mission?

(What big problem do you solve? Saving
the environment? Stopping evil robots?)

Draw Your Superhero Below!

Marie Curie- The Queen of Radioactivity!

Who was she?

Marie Curie(1867-1934) was a brilliant scientist who discovered two new elements—radium and polonium. She was the first woman to win a Nobel Prize and the only person to win it in two different sciences (Physics and Chemistry)!

Cool Fact: Marie Curie's notebooks are still radioactive—even after 100 years! Scientists have to read them wearing special suits!

How she changed the world:

Her discoveries led to X-rays, which doctors use today to look inside the human body!

Nikola Tesla - The Master of Electricity!

Who was he?

Nikola Tesla (1856-1943) was an inventor and engineer who helped bring electricity to the world! He designed the alternating current (AC) system, which powers homes, schools, and cities today!

Cool Fact: Tesla once built a giant lightning machine (called the Tesla Coil) that shot out bolts of electricity!

How he changed the world:

Without Tesla's inventions, we wouldn't have TVs, radios, or Wi-Fi!

Albert Einstein

Who was he?

Albert Einstein (1879-1955) was a scientist and mathematician who came up with E=mc², a famous equation about energy. He helped explain gravity, space, and time in a way no one had before!

Cool Fact: As a kid, Einstein's teachers thought he was slow at learning—but he became one of the smartest people ever!

How he changed the world:
His ideas led to space travel, GPS, and even lasers!

Katherine Johnson

Who was she?

Katherine Johnson (1918-2020) was a mathematician who worked for NASA. Her super-smart calculations helped launch astronauts into space and bring them back safely!

Cool Fact: She helped calculate the path for Apollo 11, the first mission to put humans on the Moon!

How she changed the world:

Her work helped make space travel possible! She also broke barriers for women and African Americans in science.

Rosalind Franklin - The Secret of DNA!

Who was she?

Rosalind Franklin (1920-1958) was a chemist who used X-rays to take the first picture of DNA, the tiny code that makes up all living things!

Cool Fact: Her DNA discoveries helped scientists understand how life works!

How she changed the world:

Her research helped lead to cures for diseases and DNA testing!

Isaac Newton - The Apple Guy!

Who was he?

Isaac Newton (1643-1727) was a scientist and mathematician who discovered gravity—the invisible force that keeps us on Earth!

Cool Fact: A falling apple inspired Newton to think about gravity and how things move in space!

How he changed the world:

His discoveries explain how planets orbit the Sun and how things move on Earth!

Louis Pasteur - The Germ Fighter!

Who was he?

Louis Pasteur (1822-1895) was a scientist who discovered that tiny germs cause diseases. He invented pasteurization, a process that keeps milk and juice fresh!

Cool Fact: Thanks to Pasteur, we have vaccines that protect us from dangerous disease!

How he changed the world:

His discoveries keep food safe and help save millions of lives!

Thank You

Thank you so much for reading my book! 📖

Out of all the books out there, you chose this one—and I'm truly grateful. 🫶

If you've made it to the end, I hope it brought you value, insight, or maybe even a little joy. ✨😊

Before you go, I have a small favor to ask:
Would you consider leaving a quick review? 📝⭐

Reviews are one of the most powerful ways to support small independent authors like me. 💪 Your honest feedback helps others discover the book, and it enables me to continue creating content that truly benefits readers like you.

Even a short review—just a sentence or two—makes a big difference. 💬✨🫶

Warmly,
Khaula Mubasher

Please go to the link or scan the QR Code below to leave a Review

https://amazon.com/review/create-review/?&asin=B0F5CKMW4K

For all other markets, find the book on the link below and leave a Review

https://mybook.to/JFcYj